Copyright © 2014 by M.W. Sonier

*Tales of the Bright Realm*
*The Peril of Astriel*
by M.W. Sonier

Printed in the United States of America

ISBN 9781498406826

All rights reserved solely by the author. The author guarantees all contents are original and do not infringe upon the legal rights of any other person or work. No part of this book may be reproduced in any form without the permission of the author. The views expressed in this book are not necessarily those of the publisher.

www.xulonpress.com

# TALES OF THE BRIGHT REALM
## The Peril of Astriel

Written by Michael W. Sonier

Edited by Marilyn B. Allen

Main character illustrations by an anonymous contributor

Maps, crest & other artwork by Michael W. Sonier

# DEDICATION

To my loving wife,
Rita
for her support in making this book a reality
and for always believing in me.

To my three (adult) children, Nicholas, André,
and Charity for their input, enthusiasm and
encouragement of their Dad; and for keeping
me young at heart.

# SPECIAL ACKNOWLEDGEMENTS

Special thanks to Marilyn Allen for her editing
prowess in reading, rereading and rereading
again (and then again), making this story
a much better read.

# TABLE OF CONTENTS

Prologue .................................................................... xv
The Bright Realm ...................................................... 19
Special Times ............................................................ 25
A Grateful People ...................................................... 29
One Dark Night ......................................................... 33
A Frightful Message .................................................. 37
Trust Me! .................................................................. 43
I Will Go! .................................................................. 49
The Gate .................................................................... 53
Let's Ride! ................................................................. 57
Brothers in Battle ...................................................... 61
No, We Head for the Pass! ........................................ 63
Fools! ........................................................................ 69
The Throwing Trees .................................................. 73
Raining Fire .............................................................. 79
Trapped! .................................................................... 85
Foiled Plans .............................................................. 91
Tense Moments ......................................................... 95
The King's Reply ...................................................... 99
A Risky Surrender? ................................................. 103
Know Your Enemy! ................................................ 109
Doubts and Fear ...................................................... 113
Well Done! .............................................................. 119
The Great Assembly ............................................... 123
Be Still! ................................................................... 129
A Tale of Deliverance ............................................. 133
Jubilation ................................................................ 141
The Decree .............................................................. 147
Epilogue .................................................................. 151

# Prologue

The evening sky had become various unnatural shades of blue, red and orange as the setting sun shone through the eerie mist lazing over the beaches of the Ivory Shores. At the entrance of his tattered shelter stood the dark lord himself, arms crossed, darkened eyes eagerly scanning the southern hills leading onto the beach where his evil encampment awaited the order to invade. Awkmos was not expecting any response from King Rowen. He waited instead for his shadowy servants to deliver to him his royal prisoner, Prince Ryen.

With the confidence and grace his royalty accorded him, Prince Ryen, accompanied by Captain Cyrus and the Hysperion, rode into the sordid camp, filled with the stench of evil. Leading his great white stallion Braam to the entrance of the shelter where the dark lord waited, he paused for a moment, still conveying his complete and supreme authority over the Bright Realm.

Slowly the prince advanced until he stood but a spear's length from the ruler of darkness. With a voice free of any fear, the prince announced firmly, "I bring word from my father Rowen, most high king of this exalted realm!" The greeting was meant as a thinly veiled reminder of his authority over the land upon which this wicked band had encamped. If it had not been for the promise of a greater deliverance, with one swift stroke of his great sword, Ryen would have at that very moment lopped the head off the shoulders of this fiendish mocker. For such was the fire that threatened to consume his breast!

## Chapter 1:
# The Bright Realm

Long, long ago, ages before our own—before mechanical devices could go under water or into space; before written messages became possible without the use of paper and ink; before a time when it became necessary to sometimes take caution with even the simplest and most basic of things—like the breathing of air or the drinking of water—there lived a king whose name was Rowen. King Rowen enjoyed the simple peace and virtue of his kingdom, known as the Bright Realm.

For as long as the king could remember, he and his son, Prince Ryen, dwelt in harmony in their beautiful castle, Tyra-Migdal (which in the ancient tongue of the kings meant *Tower of Peace*). Tyra-Migdal was built on the highest peak of the Pearl Mountains at the center of the Bright Realm. The castle's majestic walls and towers were carved out of the mountain's gleaming white stone and stood tall, overlooking the lush green valleys far below. From a distance the castle looked like it belonged in a peaceful dream.

From the High Tower of the Kings on bright days, unhindered by clouds, Rowen would have a clear view of his entire realm. Far to the west lay the Forest of Secrets, which remained a mystery to men, and mostly unexplored. From its deep woods and dark trails sprung many stories of giants and other legendary beings. To the south and southwest, far beyond the natural sight of the king, but not beyond his knowledge, lay the region of the Clans of Men, where there were endless battles for dominance of one clan over the other. Rowen longed for these people to know the peace and prosperity his realm offered. Turning his gaze to the northeast, Rowen would behold Mangled Mountain, but a day's journey from Tyra-Migdal, and the highest peak of a chain of mountains that led north. It grieved the king to know that the people of this mountain had for years refused his generous help and that to this day they believed the lies of Awkmos, the king's enemy, about him. The Valley Road along the Raffa River that ran between the two mountain chains led far north for many days' ride and then suddenly veered east before it reached the Windy Plains and the Arid Lands, where nothing had ever grown. Rowen would often think of the ancient words of the sages concerning that land—that it would one day flourish. The river emptied into the Green Sea by way of the Raffa Delta, where Tyrabel-Salbar (which in the ancient tongue meant *Harbour of Hope*) was located. To the west and northwest of the Bright Realm lay the beaches of the Ivory Shores—a long expanse of pure white sands—where the waves of the great Green Sea thundered upon the Realm's border. For years the sea had provided the kingdom with protection from invaders. Finally to the southeast, the king would see the High Peaks of Nesheer, the dwelling place of the Kanaff, the white giants of the sky, faithful servants of the Realm.

Deep in the valley below, the king would behold the wide and winding Raffa River that helped sustain life in his kingdom, for every ailing creature that would drink of its water would be restored to health and be renewed. The river's water was always cool and refreshing because it came from the snowy summits of the Realm's mountains. The water sparkled brightly like the gems of the king's royal crown, shimmering in the bright noonday sun. Filled with endless wholeness, the Raffa River and the streams of the summits also provided healing for the inhabitants of the Realm.

From the tower, the king would also have a clear view of some of the villages below. Not too far to the west he would see the Hamlet of Glowsdale, famous for its metal shaping. To the southeast and at a greater distance, sat proud Shimmerton where people bought the best fireworks in the land. Directly south was Bethardent where the most talented tailors of the Realm practiced their craft. It filled Rowen with great joy to rule over such noble and honourable people, the pride of his grand and glorious realm.

## Chapter 2:

# Special Times

On clear days, the king would climb the winding stairs to the top of the High Tower to view and appreciate the Realm. His thoughts would sometimes be carried away to a time seemingly unending. With delight, he would remember days he enjoyed swimming and fishing with his son, when the prince was only a boy. Time seemed to be still as they explored the river's banks together in search of amazing treasures. The royal pair would often spy creatures of the Realm coming to the flowing river to quench their thirst and be restored by its life-giving water. On other days they would simply lie together on its shores, basking in the warmth of the bright sun. In the clouds would form the figures of the kings of old, as Rowen would identify each one for Ryen. "There's Victor the Valiant! And look! Thoren the Truthful!" he would whisper with reverence to his son. "And there's Fabian the Faithful!" Rowen would sometimes wonder to himself if one day his own figure would appear in the clouds of the Bright Realm, alongside the ancient rulers.

"Ah! Such special times!" Rowen thought to himself on this day, as he leaned against the white stoney wall of the high tower, looking over the Realm. The king smiled at the pleasant memories, a welcomed relief from the thoughts that had been troubling him recently. One thing gave the king his greatest joy: the sharing of his rule with his son, Prince Ryen. Rowen's love for his kingdom was surpassed only by his love for his beloved son.

On this day, however, thoughts of his son jolted the musing king back to the matters at hand, to the great trouble that had come upon the Realm. Awkmos, his archenemy, had invaded Rowen's peaceful realm and threatened to take over the reign of his beloved land and its people. The dark lord had set up his evil encampment on the sands of the Ivory Shores, and the thought of this was almost unbearable to Rowen. The king held in his hand the rolled-up scroll, an ultimatum Awkmos had delivered just three days earlier. Struck once again by these troubling thoughts, he slumped forward against the white, rocky wall of the tower and let out a long grievous sigh.

## Chapter 3:

# A Grateful People

In the villages below, the king's subjects loved their king as their very own father and were deeply devoted to him. They served him eagerly and with gladness of heart. Like a loving father, King Rowen had always cared affectionately and ruled justly over them. They felt deeply indebted to him for their healthy and prosperous lives and were extremely grateful. "The very creatures of the woodland and forests revere the king!" the people would say. "The creatures even stop to bow to the king and prince as they travel the wooded areas on their great horses!" they exclaimed in wonder as they met in the public squares.

Their festive nights would always end with the Realm's best known blessing, "King Rowen forever! Prince Ryen forevermore!" The creatures of the realm would also enjoy their own festivities, dancing and rejoicing, each with their own kind. Their stomachs never knew the pangs of hunger, and when they were ailing, they would drink of the water of the river and be restored. Every such creature that would drink would also be filled with the knowledge of their king's goodness and a desire to be of service to him.

New *arrivers* to the Bright Realm would always be welcomed by King Rowen himself in a special ceremony held twice every year in the castle's court. The king wanted each newcomer to feel like he or she belonged. They would come from other lands, some from beyond the Green Sea where Awkmos, the dark lord, had his domain. His hand was exceptionally cruel and without mercy. Many who dared an escape from his dominion would be recaptured and treated ever more harshly, becoming examples to others with thoughts of flight. Those who succeeded, however, and entered Rowen's realm, were greeted with great joy.

The arrivers would bathe in the cool water of the Raffa River, and in time their bodies would be healed. They would drink from the springs of the mountains, and in time their minds would mend. As time passed, the newcomers would forget the cruel hardships they had suffered by the evil hand of Awkmos. As time passed, the life they had left behind would become just a sad memory, like a bad dream from which they had finally awakened. Their hard years of toil and slavery would melt away like snow in the warmth of spring. As time passed, the newcomers would be changed, becoming ageless in body, youthful in mind, and in need of less and less sleep: a few of the many amazing mysteries of the Bright Realm.

## Chapter 4:

# One Dark Night

Three days earlier, however, on a dark and stormy night, the evil lord Awkmos landed with his wicked hosts on the Ivory Shores, which formed part of the western border of King Rowen's Bright Realm. For ages the Green Sea had separated the Bright Realm from the evil lord's dark land. The sea had also provided safety for the kingdom and its people. Few were aware, however, that it was fear of Astriel the Radiant, the king's sword of legend, that kept Awkmos and his dark forces away. Even fewer expected he would one day dare to lead his evil hordes to the shores of Rowen's great realm.

The king, however, had known for many years about his enemy's desire. Sophim, the great sage, had long ago foretold the Day of Darkness that would overshadow the Bright Realm. Yes, the king knew the desire of Awkmos to invade his kingdom and take over his land. Such knowledge could not be hidden from the kings of the Realm, but Rowen knew not Awkmos' plan.

On this day, as far as the eye could see, the white sandy expanse of the Ivory Shores became covered by a dark shadow. Like thick clouds of locusts, the black hordes swarmed the imperial shores, concealing them with a heavy shroud of evil. Everywhere, tents and shelters of every kind were being built. Billows of black smoke streamed into the clear night sky as the shimmering light of the growing number of campfires spotted the shores, seemingly as numerous as the stars themselves. The putrid stench of spoiling foods and other decay had begun to fill the air.

To Awkmos, however, these were the pleasurable sights, sounds and smells of his approaching victory over his long-time enemy. The dark ruler deeply despised King Rowen for the mercy he granted to the many who escaped the wicked lands to seek refuge in the Bright Realm. "His kindness has made him weak and vulnerable," reflected Awkmos in the dark recesses of his hateful mind. "For years I have desired to tear this land from the pitiful hands of this kindly king!" he hissed vengefully to himself. As Awkmos raised his mighty black blade, he shouted across the evil encampment, "On this day Rowen will fall! His beloved realm will be mine! And I will finally have my long awaited revenge!" The night sky darkened even more as if some force were responding to these evil declarations. The air suddenly grew cold as a fowl mist rolled into the encampment.

## Chapter 5:

# A Frightful Message

The journey from the evil encampment to the castle gates took several days for the messenger of the dark lord. Though travel had been made quicker by the well maintained Valley Road along the Realm's Raffa River, the distance was still formidable. The heinous messenger could not have undertaken such travels, however, without an official Realm Escort. A venture without such accompaniment would have been foolhardy, ending in certain death for the lone traveller, for the king exercised full authority over his kingdom.

The courier became crippled with fear upon arriving at Tyra-Migdal, King Rowen's castle. Standing before its massive gates as they were lowered, his instinct was to flee, like a frightened mouse. The gates would surely squash him like the insect that he was if they were suddenly to fall. Even more frightening was the thought of standing before this great and powerful ruler. Only fear of having to face his dark master kept him from fleeing, however. The wretched messenger deeply resented his errand and silently begrudged his lord's orders, and even his master's very existence.

As the courier entered the inner courts of Tyra-Migdal, a palace guard quickly escorted the knob-kneed creature into the presence of the king, to whom the messenger finally delivered the all-important communication from Awkmos. In unhurried fashion, Rowen broke the seal and carefully unrolled the scroll as the shadowy figure eagerly looked on. His attempts to avoid Rowen's piercing gaze were in vain, however, for in the eyes of the king he caught a brief glimpse of his own doom. This brief and unexpected insight revealed to him the futility of the plans of his evil master. The dark messenger, faced with this new knowledge, was filled with sudden dread.

*A Frightful Message*

The words hurriedly scratched on the piece of soiled parchment paper were few and lacked all common greetings, but the foreboding message was clear. In dark and defiant strokes it read:

## SURRENDER YOUR KINGDON TO ME NOW, OR IN THREE DAYS HAVE IT TORN FROM YOUR GRASP!

Below the threatening text was scrawled the sinister name: AWKMOS.

Turning sharply to the on-looking messenger, the king's response was simple, yet filled with royal authority, "Tell your leader to expect an answer from me speedily!" The strength of the sudden response startled the messenger. Reeling in sudden fright, he stumbled backwards, almost falling flat on the marble floor. The palace guard quickly guided the flailing courier from the presence of the king, down the long bright hallway and the circular marble stairs unto the castle's inner courts again, and through the main gates to the awaiting escort.

Once alone, Rowen sighed deeply as his gaze went over to his son Ryen, who patiently waited for his father to confirm what the prince already strongly suspected. "We knew the Day of Darkness would one day be upon us!" said the king grimly. "Lord Awkmos has finally made his move to take over the rule of our glorious realm," he added. The king's gaze was as sullen as his voice. For a long while there was only silence between father and son as they both felt the weight of this disturbing message.

As Ryen searched his father's eyes, the prince began to catch glimpses of the glory of their kingdom from ages past as it unfolded in the king's mind. Every challenge! Every battle! Every oracle the kings trusted! Every victory! When finally his father spoke, instead of the sullenness that had weighed on the king's mind, Ryen heard renewed hope and strength in his father's voice. "My son! We must look to the former years for our hope. We must remember the words of Sophim from long ago!" Speaking with renewed hope and determination, the king gradually stood, exclaiming, "Let us renew our hope! The time has finally come for the fulfillment of the plan of old concerning the Bright Realm! . . . Come, my son! We must make haste!"

*A Frightful Message*

The sound of their footsteps disappeared down the long, bright hallway. Echoing back were the words of agreement of the prince, "Yes, father! Let us renew our hope indeed! The time HAS finally come!"

## Chapter 6:

# Trust Me!

Rowen squandered no time calling his royal scribe to his chambers, where the king and his son were waiting. Shafts of bright morning light from two tall, stone-edged windows struck the marble floor of the chamber at an angle, climbing part way up a large elegant tapestry that hung on the opposing wall. It would have been just another perfect morning in the Realm had it not been for the serious matter at hand. "Today, you must double your vigilance as you record my words, my dear Graphis!" confided Rowen to his beloved scribe.

"Yes, my Lord!" The scribe gracefully nodded his acknowledgement to the king as he carefully set the inkwell and parchment paper before him on the scribal table. He sat quietly, waiting with customary patience for the king to begin.

Graphis was a tall slender man with a protruding chin, pointy nose and light coloured hair tied back and resembling the long gallant tail of one of the king's noble horses. King Rowen, on the other hand, was a man of medium height, broad and massive at the chest, with legs, arms and hands to match. His long dark locks rested heavily on his shoulders. One would hardly have expected the two men to become friends. Yet, they had become very close friends. Over the years, Graphis had also become one of the king's most trusted advisers. Through many meetings and long hours of discussion, the royal scribe had studied his lord well. On this day, Graphis noted an unusual malaise which the king could not entirely conceal as he spoke—a tension to which the trusted scribe was not accustomed in his meetings with his king and good friend. Preparing to fulfill his royal duty, the scribe shifted nervously in his seat, wondering about what could possibly be troubling the king. Nothing would have prepared the scribe for what he was about to learn. Nothing ever could have!

The scribe became visibly shaken as he carefully and skillfully recorded every word the king gave him to write. From the mere inscription of words and thoughts, his scribal skills had developed into a form of intuitive art, every message a work of precision, every scroll a work of creation.

After he blew away the drying dust from the piece of parchment, the deeply concerned scribe examined it carefully, once again satisfied with its beauty. Cautiously rolling up the scroll, his hands trembled as he handed it to Rowen. Perceiving his good friend's concern, the king gently said, "Do not worry, Graphis!" The king's words stirred the royal scribe from the numbness that had settled over his mind, penetrating his swirling thoughts.

"My Lord?" The scribe's few words betrayed his agitation as his voice trembled with doubt. Taking a step back, he searched the king's gaze for reassurance concerning what he had just recorded.

"As you have always trusted your king, trust me in this as well, dear friend!" Rowen added. The king's words were solemn, yet in his eyes

Graphis perceived a deep well of unmovable confidence, the strength of a king of ancient days. In his heart Graphis felt his hope renewed. Like the unveiling of a mystery long awaiting to be revealed, the faithful scribe wondered in amazement at this high king, a descendent of the royal race of men. Taking another step back, and with all the gracefulness of his slender form, the scribe silently bowed before this one of old.

## Chapter 7:

# I Will Go!

"This matter is far too important, Father!" passionately exclaimed the prince. "I will deliver this message to Awkmos myself!" The king knew his son well. Unlike his father, the prince was of taller height and of medium build, with shoulders not as broad, but still rugged and powerful, and of muscular limbs with a grip of steel. His eyes displayed a deep kindness and an ageless wisdom, yet were filled with an unyielding determination.

Rowen knew very well that Ryen would not have the matter any other way. Yet his love for his son would not allow him to remain silent, nor without argument. "But the way will be treacherous, my son!" the king protested as he moved towards the tall window nearest him, into the warmth of the sun. "Our enemy has indeed become bold!" he continued vainly. "By now he will have his spies covering the Realm, taking on many forms!"

The prince recognized the wisdom of his father's words but remained firm in his resolution. He would not be denied the opportunity to once again serve and defend the people and the realm that he loved just as dearly as did his father. Turning towards his son, the king looked upon his countenance for a long moment . . . and marvelled! Standing in all splendour before him as in a dream was a valiant prince of old, in blazing armour, with raised shield and drawn sword. From his mouth came forth the battle cry of Astriel the Radiant, thunderous and mighty. From his heart shone forth the pure light of hope in amazing brilliance. His courage was undaunted and his strength unequalled. In wonder and amazement, the king bowed before his son, and at that moment, yielded to the will of the ages.

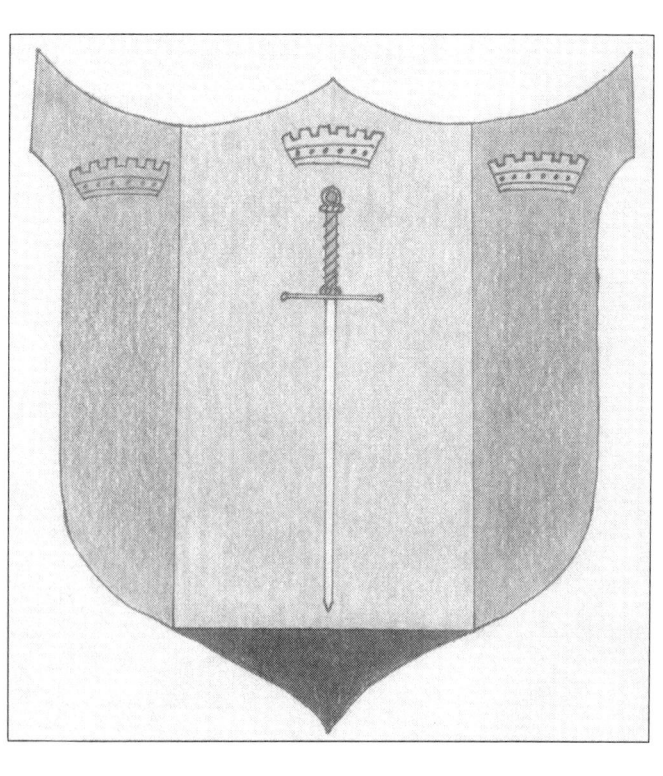

## Chapter 8:

# The Gate

"Go, my son, . . . and take with you the One Hundred, our finest and most valiant warriors. Take with you the Hysperion!" The king's gaze had become overshadowed with concern as the prince turned to leave the royal chambers. "MY SON!" The sudden words resounded in a dying echo throughout his chamber. The urgency in the words stopped Ryen in his gait and he slowly turned to meet his father's sullen look. "Return to me in haste! . . . For my heart quakes at the thought of the loss of you!" In a moment of visual embrace, King and Prince, father and son, beheld each other. No other words needed uttering. Ryen once again turned to leave, but less eagerly this time, almost painfully.

The prince parted with his father's blessing as he sped quietly down the hallway all too familiar to him. Ryen slowed his steps as waking dreams passed before his eyes, dreams of himself as a boy, running, playing, and hiding in those secret recesses of this majestic castle in which he had grown up. He counted the number of steps he took to reach the spiralling staircase. "Exactly 64!" he thought to himself in amusement. "That's the number of steps it always took Father to reach the staircase as well," he mused. The rising mists of sorrow that was threatening to rob his heart of joy and hope soon yielded to the comforting memories of these waking dreams. The prince smiled pleasantly at these thoughts as he followed the circular staircase down to his company of men waiting for him at the main gate of the castle.

The large iron gate of the castle had already been raised and the draw bridge lowered. The surface of the draw bridge, smooth and gleaming, had the glassy appearance of a frozen lake. The underside was thickly laden with the strongest of metals from the royal foundries. The protective passageway was hoisted by a sct of three

*The Gate*

---

large chains on either side. When raised, the outside of the draw bridge displayed the royal crest in the form of a giant shield of the army of the Bright Realm. From the top of the shield almost to the bottom, the middle was blue like the clear summer sky, with the green of prosperity on the left, and the brown of the earth on the right. Down the middle, as if standing guard over the Realm, was the image of Astriel the Radiant, protector of ancient days. Also displayed in the royal crest, at the top, were three crowns: a crown of silver in one corner of the shield, a crown of bronze in the other corner, and a third of gold hovering over Astriel. Finally, the bottom of the crest was coloured in black. Few were those who understood the meaning of this colour and why such a dark blemish would even appear on the glorious crest of the Bright Realm. Together, however, the royal symbols stood as a reminder to all who entered the Bright Realm and Tyra-Migdal through the gate that they were beyond all harm. The castle and its gate were impenetrable, the great stone walls guarded night and day. And Astriel the Protector stood always at attention.

## Chapter 9:

# Let's Ride!

Word of this most important mission had quickly reached the Hysperion, the king's One Hundred, the High Guard. These knights had already assembled and mounted their magnificent horses, all white in colour, the finest in the Realm. Their warrior steeds were descendants of the Mighty Bronnam, greatest war horse that has ever served the king. Each was trained for battle by his rider, but none was mastered by him, for these horses were much more than simple beasts of war. A closely knit kinship would develop between mount and rider which required no mastery. Both were keenly aware of the purpose of their duty. They were partners in service of their king, members of the High Guard of the glorious Realm of the kings of old.

The roots of trust between man and beast would grow deep, like those of the kingdom's great elms. Such was the kinship that existed between horse and rider that one learned to perceive the thoughts and intentions of the other, and to even understand each other's language.

Today, there would be no gleaming of the brilliant armour of either horse or rider in the bright morning sun, for their mission required haste and stealth. However, shields bearing the royal symbols were readied and swords drawn and raised to hail the beloved leader of the Hysperion as he approached. "Prince Ryen forever!" the Guard cried loudly as one. Smiling in response, the prince drew and raised his own sword as he made his way through the formation that greeted him so affectionately. At the end of this formation, his own great stallion Braam, chief of all horses, waited with braided mane, sporting eyelets resembling the wings of an eagle ready to take flight. Braam's saddle sparkled with polished leather, brass, and silver.

Fastened to one side of the ornate saddle was a long, slender object, wrapped in common cloth, which drew no particular attention to itself. The

*Let's Ride!*

object could have passed for a travelling item, of use for the long trek ahead. Passing before the High Guard, Ryen paused before his valiant horse and whispered gently in his ear, "Once again, my faithful Braam, we ride in service of king and kingdom!" The horse whinnied softly in anticipation, acknowledging his master's words, sole rider of this chiefest of steeds.

In one graceful motion, the prince was in his saddle. Drawing his sword again, he raised it high toward the sky. "Forever the king and Astriel!" he shouted to his men, his strong voice resounding off the castle walls.

"Forever the king and Astriel" the Hysperion returned as one and just as strongly.

"Cyrus!" commanded the prince with authority. "We must ride immediately! Our journey is long and we have little time!"

## Chapter 10:

# Brothers in Battle

Cyrus, the captain of the Hysperion, rode slightly higher in the saddle than the prince. His curly black locks of hair (with a bushy black beard to match) blew in the wind as they rode. His powerful physique and cunning skills as a warrior had certainly earned the respect of the men under his command. But it was his utter devotion to the king and prince that won the deepest affection of the Guard.

In turn, the prince trusted Cyrus and the High Guard with his very life's breath. Many were the battles to which he had ridden with these valiant warriors, and with as many victories he had returned with them. Each member of the Hysperion had become a trusted friend. Some of his closest were Rubriel, the gentle master of horses, Adriel, the patient crafter of leather, and Cantriel, the gifted shaper of metals. His closest and dearest friend, however, was Cyrus, most valiant captain of the High Guard. Besides Ryen himself, no warrior in the king's entire army was as brave a defender of the kingdom and truer to its virtues than Cyrus.

In turn, all the Hysperion, along with the entire army of the Realm, esteemed none above the prince. Every member of the High Guard was selected not simply on the basis of his proven skills as a warrior, but especially because of his devotion to the king and prince. Each would give his life without warning or hesitation in service of ruler and kingdom. It was certainly not a lack of confidence in these brave and valiant men that had urged Ryen to insist on being the one to deliver to Awkmos the message of the king.

## Chapter 11:
# No, We Head for the Pass!

The brave company moved urgently down the winding mountain road. The royal banner, displaying a sword and three crowns, beat the wind in defiance of enemy spies. These lay hidden, concealed by the darkness of rocky crags and crevices, and in the shadows of the trees and underbrush. The king's horses were among the noblest of steeds: fast, agile and eager to answer to their rider's bidding. For hours at a time, the horsemen never slowed their gruelling pace, pausing only to fill their drinking bottles and to allow their horses a brief rest and a drink. The life-giving water from the brook was cool and refreshing, reviving the life of both rider and mount. The smallest of drinks from the Realm's springs was all that was necessary to renew their vigour.

Continuing onward towards their awaiting foe, the Guard needed no prodding. All were keenly aware of the urgent nature of their perilous mission. The sun had set hours before the party stopped to set up camp at the end of their first day's journey. In spite of having become accustomed to such gruelling treks, both man and beast were in need of much rest.

Long after the company had settled in for the night, the prince sat with Cyrus around the campfire. Their faces were flushed with the orange light from the fire. Ryen's voice suddenly broke the stillness of the cool night. "We must reach the white shores at the edge of the kingdom by sunset two days hence!" confided the prince. "The dark lord awaits us there!"

The captain's keen eyes met his master's. "My Lord!" he replied suspiciously. "Even if we were to press on without food or rest for two full days, the borders of the Realm would still fall far beyond the reach of such a valiant trek!" The captain paused briefly in thought, looking into the flames. Turning his attention back to the prince, the captain shrewdly concluded, "You do not intend on continuing on the Valley Road along the Raffa River, do you, my Lord?"

The prince was pleased with the captain's keen insight. "No, my friend! For that path would lead us north for several days still, almost to the furthest edge of the kingdom. We would then have to turn east for more days still before reaching the camp of the enemy. No, we would not arrive at the appointed time to deliver the king's message!" The prince paused for a moment, looking away as if gazing into an unsure future. In his heart he knew this was part of the plan of the enemy, and suspected its purpose. Turning his gaze back to his beloved captain, he added, "We must take the path over Mangled Mountain!"

"It is as I thought then!" replied Cyrus, not surprised, yet still unsettled by the sudden news from his master. "The people of the mountain are unruly brutes. Never have they inclined to your father's rule! . . . But already do you know all this, my Lord!" More uneasy silence followed.

By now, the prince had turned his gaze back to the blazing fire. His eyes were peering past its flames, however, into an age long out of memory. The prince began to quietly sing. As the loyal captain listened, his heart began to be strangely stirred. He marvelled at the mysterious melody caressing his ears like the gentle strokes of the softest feather or like the settling of a fresh morning mist. For long ages past this simple song had been lost to men, wandering in obscurity and forgotten. On this night, however, the ancient song had been revived, captivating its listener, bringing hope and encouragement to his heart.

> Realm of the ages, white shores overridden
> Mists of darkness, evil has risen
> Mountains resisting, opposing, defending
> On this day defeated, no longer dissenting
> Forevermore bowing to ruler and king

The enchanting sounds of these melodic lines disappeared quietly on the cool breeze of the Realm and into the night. "My friend," reassured Ryen looking over at the captain after a moment, "we must trust the ancient words. This darkness will not end in our loss!" Stoking the fire with the last few pieces of firewood, the prince prepared his bed. "In the morning," he confidently concluded, "we will head for the pass at the very

*No, We Head for the Pass!*

---

top of Mangled Mountain! Once we get through the Gate of Wanderers and reach the eastern base of the mountain, from there, the Ivory Shores are but a day's journey. . . . Let us sleep now, for we will surely need the rest for the journey which lies ahead!"

## Chapter 12:

# Fools!

"So the fools have fallen for my trap!" the raspy voice of the dark lord rang out from his tattered looking shelter as he paced the dirt floor back and forth like a caged animal. The air inside was clouded with the smoke of lanterns burning in each corner of the tent. The lighting devices were fuelled with a foul mixture of various oils and animal fats. The eyes of the returning messenger pained from the sting of the heavy smoke. He gasped for clean air as he reported to his foreboding master, who seemed unaffected by the thick cloud of fumes. Awkmos revelled in the good news he was hearing. "Leave me now, Fiend!" he barked as he ordered his slave out of his shelter. "You shall be rewarded for these most delightful tidings in due time!" The creature had expected a more immediate reward, however. If he was not given one now, before leaving the shelter, the slave knew none would ever be offered. So he decided to keep to himself the future he had perceived in the eyes of the king concerning the futility of his evil master's plans.

Once the messenger had gone, Awkmos sat quietly by himself, remembering with fiendish delight his meeting with the people of Mangled Mountain not many days before. He recalled the alliance he had formed with these wicked folks, and the promise of a shared rule once Rowen was defeated. The dark ruler sneered deceitfully, exposing broken yellow teeth. He had no intention of sharing his rule with anything else living or dead. He would use the mountain people to capture the king's son and kill his men. With his son in captivity, Rowen would have no hidden thoughts of resistance or of any other intentions of defence. Furthermore, the people of the mountain would simply have to bow to his rule or perish by the wielded weapons of his army.

"Yes! My plan is perfect!" the malicious one thought to himself as a quiet, sinister laugh escaped his venomous lips. "Soon I will be sole ruler over this realm that for much too long has eluded my grasp! Then I will be supreme ruler over all!" The quietness of the night air was suddenly filled with the sound of his vicious laugh.

## Chapter 13:
# The Throwing Trees

The winding trail up Mangled Mountain to the Gate of Wanderers was steep and perilous. It was strictly a mere footpath worn into the mountainside by all that passed that way—men, beasts and other living creatures. On one side, the walls of the mountain were sharp and jagged, ready to tear into the flesh of rider and mount. On the other, the cliffs were steep and deadly. One forgetful step would end in certain death. Also, the large roots of the infamous *throwing trees* jutted out of the mountainside and across the path, making passage even more treacherous. These trees became known thus by both lowlanders and mountain people alike because of the stories from the occasional traveller of the mountain trail. The tales tell of strong gusting of winds, during which the large, low hanging branches of the trees would sway dangerously, catching unsuspecting travellers and throwing them down the mountainside, into the ravine far below. Anyone travelling the path had to be on constant guard.

The prince, however, had long ago learned the truth concerning the throwing trees, that they were actually creatures of intelligence, able to talk to one another, and hated the intrusion of travellers on the mountain path. By listening carefully, the informed traveller would hear the ancient language of the trees, separate from the sounds of the howling wind: the distinct deep groans, vibrating whispers, and high pitched shrieks. Ryen also knew that, unlike the mountain people, these *Trees* had at one time, long ago, declared their allegiance to the ancient kings of the Realm. On this day, however, Ryen wondered to himself, "Will the Mountain Trees still recognize their allegiance? Will they acknowledge the authority of a Prince of the Bright Realm?"

Not wanting to risk needless danger for his men, Ryen rode on ahead, leaving Cyrus and the Guard behind on the trail. "If I have not returned in an hour hence," he instructed the captain, "you will have to find another way to deliver the message to Awkmos!"

Carefully approaching the edge of the rightful domain of the Trees, which had already begun to stir at the approach of the lone traveller, the prince descended from his great horse Braam and stood tall. Ryen then confidently declared in the tongue of the kings of old (a language which all living creatures of the Realm understood), "I am Prince Ryen, son of Rowen, High King of the Bright Realm! You are bound by your allegiance to the kings of old to suffer the passage of me and every member of my company on the mountain path!" The prince had to speak loudly to be heard over the sound of the howling wind as it blew his long black hair across his face.

Tense moments passed as the surprised Mountain Trees groaned and moaned, shook and swayed, convening among themselves! The prince waited patiently! Then, as the Trees settled, the deep rumblings of a well-defined voice responded just as confidently, "I am Tangledroots, chief of the Mountain Trees! Long ago the Trees of the mountain had honoured the rule of the

High King over our domain, and do still honour this rule today! We would gladly suffer the passage of any lowlander who comes in the king's name to travel the heights of the mountain trail!" The voice was slow and resolute, coarse yet clear, with the innate authority of a chief as it continued. "Well do you speak the language of the olden kings, but how can we Trees know you are who you *claim* to be, my young lowlander? Furthermore, we need to know what is the purpose of these most exceedingly rare travels of yours and of your company's on this high mountain path, for it is our sworn duty to protect it?" questioned the chief of the Trees justifiably.

"In reply to your very valid query, my lord Tree, behold the signet ring of the rulers of the Bright Realm, one of only three that have ever been crafted!" responded Ryen respectfully as he removed the riding glove from his right hand, displaying the elegant ring on his pointing finger. The ornately crafted ring, shaped to fit the finger of its bearer, was in identical resemblance of the king's sword, Astriel the Radiant, including a bright red gem. The Trees shook and trembled in awe at the sight of it, groaning and moaning to one another, for the ring served to confirm the truth of this traveller's words. "As for the purpose of our passage, it concerns the evil encampment on the Ivory Shores, the presence of which I am persuaded you are already aware, and requires our haste! We would not have chosen such a dangerous route if it was not otherwise!" the prince said, concluding his reply.

Ryen needed not wait very long for Tangledroots' response, as chief of the Mountain Trees. "Ah, my young lord Prince! The Trees of the mountain bow to you!", which they did for a reverent moment. The sounds of creaking and cracking joined with the noises of the blowing wind. After they had again straightened, with additional creaking and cracking, Tangledroots continued, "Safe passage you and your company are granted through our domain. Every Tree will pull back its roots from across the path and refrain from swaying its branches. May your steps be sure and your path safe! Beware, however, upon reaching the higher trail! There are beings there that still have not acknowledged the rule of your father, the High King!" With these words of both blessing and warning, Prince Ryen and the High Guard were able to continue their trek up the narrow path of Mangled Mountain. The reverence of the moment when tree and traveller encountered on the trail, as the company rode by, was forever etched on the mind of each warrior.

## Chapter 14:

# Raining Fire

After hours of slow, painful ascent, no longer able to ride any further, the High Guard continued their trek in a single file up the winding and still narrowing mountain trail. Yet, not one member of the heroic band ever once questioned the decision of their master to pass this way.

"Cyrus!" the prince said decisively. "We will make camp tonight at the Great Gate, just over the summit of the mountain! Pass this word down the line to each member of the Guard!" he ordered. Without hesitation, the captain spoke the words to the guard behind him, and he to the one behind him. The message became fainter as it travelled down the line to the very end.

Darkness had again already settled on the single file of men as they approached the summit of the mountain, which in recent ages was always covered in snow, and where the wind raged constantly. The path near the summit had widened slightly, creating a natural basin shape which allowed for the carving of the pass out of the thick wall of rock before them. The pass itself was a tunnel large enough for man and beast to enter, after which lay a cave that could accommodate a large enough company. Tunnel and cave were the result of years of erosion from days when the mountain's snowy caps did not stay year round. The coming of the mountain people, along with the increasing darkness of evil, caused the mountain to grow cold and merciless, like its new inhabitants. On either side of the path leading up to the tunnel, the mountain walls continued to rise, but not as steep as before. Until now, the watchful eyes of the company had only noticed signs of the people of the mountain. Their trek to the summit had been precarious, but otherwise safe and uneventful.

The howling wind whipped the snow around sharply, blowing the frozen crystals like little darts of ice into their eyes. The Guard shielded their eyes from the painful projectiles. All this time, the leery captain had been carefully examining their surroundings. Crying out to the prince above the sound of the blowing wind, he exclaimed cautiously, "If I were to stage an attack on my enemy, it would be at the top of these cliffs!" The blowing snow caused the captain to turn away, shielding his eyes from the blinding ice darts. After a moment, when he dared to once again face the icy menace, he continued loudly, "An unsuspecting company would have little warning, and even less with which to conceal themselves. They would be at the mercy of their attackers!" he added. The blinking prince, his own eyes straining to scour their surroundings, nodded his acknowledgement to the concerned captain.

As if the exchange between the brave leaders had been overheard over the sound of the howling winds, wild, shrieking cries suddenly erupted from above. Within seconds, the freezing air surrounding the Guard was filled with chilling screams of war and the alarming clamour of an enemy's attack. Blazing projectiles of every kind began to rain down upon the Hysperion. The dark night sky suddenly became ablaze with flaming arrows, spears and fireballs. How these savages of the mountain managed to mount such a brutal fiery assault in such circumstances was a mystery to the company. One could only guess they were being assisted by some other evil.

The prince and captain reacted instinctively. "Into the cave!" they shouted loudly to their men, waving them on as each man raised his shield to protect himself and his horse as best as he could from the blazing assault. Every man knew that safety from the savage attack lay within the cave. Every man also knew that upon entering the tunnel, the entire Guard would be trapped inside. Further attacks would simply follow from either end of the pass. They knew, furthermore, that the vulnerable Guard could not survive such a brutal and merciless assault for much longer out in the open. So, enter the tunnel they had to, and did. One by one, shielding themselves from the ongoing attack, horse and rider scurried in, into a trap from which there was no apparent escape!

## Chapter 15:

# Trapped!

"My Lord," Cyrus called out from the dimly lit passage, reporting back to the prince. "The entire guard now lies safely inside, but not all. We have suffered the loss of three of our men and two horses!" It grieved Ryen deeply to receive such sad tidings. His anger with the mountain people burned greatly because of it. "Also, my lord, the entrance of the tunnel is being blocked with wood and stubble, such as the barbarians are able to find!" the captain added with concern. "I believe they are wanting to fill the cave with smoke to force us out. If we attempt to flee, we will certainly perish by the hand of our enemy! And if we remain, we will also surely perish from the fire's poisonous cloud!"

The courageous captain's gaze was sullen, searching his master's for answers or solutions, and most of all for hope as he continued his dismal report. "I have ordered a search of the entire tunnel and passageway for perhaps another way of escape, but none appears to exist!" he added. The dismaying captain turned to lunge with his sword at the stone wall of the cave as if to repel an approaching invisible enemy. The darkness around him lit up with the brief flash of metal colliding with stone. "Has hope abandoned us on this day of greatest need, to perish at the hands of this wickedness?" the brave captain shouted in frustration. For it is possible for even the bravest of warriors to fall victim to despair.

Shifting his attention from their apparent doom to the esteemed captain, and with the greatest gentleness, Ryen softly pleaded, "Do not surrender to the despair that would lay siege to your heart, my dear Cyrus, for though hope may not always be perceived, it is always near! Remember the words of the ancient song, and remember my words to you when I said, '*This darkness will not end in our loss!*'"

The captain settled, in wonder at the far-reaching depth of the hope he beheld in his kind master at that moment. The ancient wisdom of the son of the king reached into his despairing heart, reviving hope and renewing his strength. "Forgive me for despairing, my lord!" he quietly replied in humble esteem of the prince and after a moment of reflexion. "May the grace that sustains your heart also forever sustain mine and guard it from ever despairing again!" the captain quietly exclaimed.

The inspiring moment of admiration and rekindled hope was abruptly brought to an end by another disturbance coming from outside the cave, sudden thundering blasts and blinding light. "This attack comes from the very summit of the mountain!" reported a surprised guard to the unsuspecting prince and captain. The ongoing blasts became mingled with cries of panic and the sounds of a horn blowing a call of retreat. Their savage attackers had given up their assault and were fleeing in fear, but of what, of whom? The brave company prepared a hurried defense against whatever force that had routed the barbarians and overtaken their mountain.

The thick smoke outside the cave quickly dissipated and the only remaining sound was that of the howling winds. Appearing mysteriously in the entrance of the tunnel was the dark image of a tall, solemn figure. The curious looking figure appeared to be wearing a long woollen garb and a tall, wide-rimmed pointy hat, and had in hand a long wooden staff of sorts. His face was partly concealed by the headdress, but also by a very long, yet full grayish-white beard wrapped around his neck as a woollen scarf for warmth against the bitter cold. The eyes of this unexpected "guest" still shone as fire, lighting his snowy brow and red cheeks. "Greetings, friends!" called a deep but cheerful voice. "In a bit of a predicament, are we?" he questioned amusingly.

"Have you come as a friend of the Realm or as a foe commissioned by the enemy?" enquired the unsuspecting captain dutifully. The Guard held its defensive position, unmoved by this seemingly powerful stranger, yet wondering by what force he could possibly have defeated the savage mountain people. Their wonder quickly turned to astonishment at the sudden cry of joy that erupted from their prince. Ryen's eyes and ears had confirmed for him what his heart had already been suspecting. Their deliverance had come from the hand of one upon whom the eyes of the prince had not rested since he sat as a child at his father's side. On that day long ago, the memory of this figure of ancient times was forever etched upon his young mind. "Sophim!" the prince shouted with delight as he welcomed their rugged looking deliverer.

Suspicion had turned to surprise, and surprise to wonder as the Hysperion beheld for the first time one whose deeds and renown they had learned of, as boys, through ancient tales and of whose legend they sang in ancient strains— the sage of old who one day came to dwell in the Bright Realm, to be of service to its kings. Before them stood Sophim, wisest of sages of ancient days and humble servant of the most high king.

## Chapter 16:
# Foiled Plans

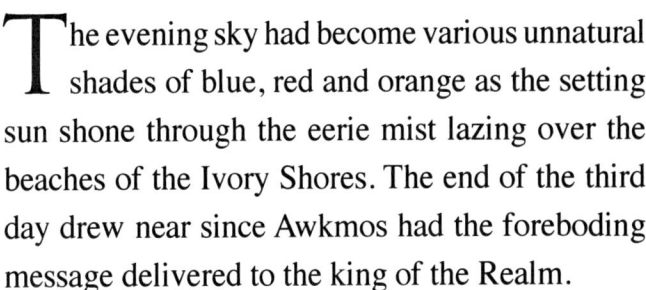

The evening sky had become various unnatural shades of blue, red and orange as the setting sun shone through the eerie mist lazing over the beaches of the Ivory Shores. The end of the third day drew near since Awkmos had the foreboding message delivered to the king of the Realm.

At the entrance of his tattered shelter stood the dark lord, arms crossed, darkened eyes eagerly scanning the southern hills leading onto the beach where his evil encampment awaited the order to invade. Awkmos was not expecting any response from Rowen. He waited instead for his shadowy servants to deliver to him his royal prisoner, Prince Ryen, and gloated at the thought of the approaching success of the evil plan he had so carefully devised.

The sudden blast of a warning horn quickly jolted Awkmos out of his slumbering thoughts! Running up to him and throwing himself at his soiled boots was the twisted form of a retched messenger, trembling like a frightened dog before a ruthless master. "A company of riders arrives, my lord!" Awkmos was delighted in the long awaited news. "It is the prince!" stammered the servant as he continued. But before the dark lord could celebrate this glorious victory, the messenger fearfully added with trembling voice, "He comes with his guard and of his own will. He rides into our camp not in defeat as your prisoner, but as the exalted son of the most high king!"

Awkmos was instantly outraged at the sudden realization of his failed plans with the mountain people. He did not have time at this moment, however, to dwell on this lack of success, even if a seething anger dropped to the pit of his being at these unexpected and most unpleasant tidings. With the viciousness of a fearsome beast, the dark lord suddenly struck out at the cowering servant bowed before him. The pitiful creature let out a yelp of agony as he scurried off through

## Foiled Plans

the legs of the gathering mop. Awkmos knew he needed to quickly gather his wits and prepare to meet with his most unwelcomed guest. He did not want to convey the slightest grain of surprise at the unexpected arrival of the prince.

## Chapter 17:

# Tense Moments

With the confidence and grace his royalty accorded him, Prince Ryen, accompanied by Captain Cyrus and the Hysperion, rode into the sordid camp filled with the stench of evil. Leading his great white horse Braam to the entrance of the shelter where the dark lord waited, he paused for a moment, still conveying his complete authority over the shores of the Bright Realm. Next to the prince sat Captain Cyrus, mounted on his own valiant steed. Behind the two men had formed a row of five royal archers, sitting at attention in their saddles, with ornately carved birch bows in hand. A quiver full of golden feathered arrows hung at each of their sides, where their free hands rested, ready.

After a brief moment, Ryen dismounted in regal fashion, leaning in toward Braam, as if to adjust his bridal. "Stand ready, my faithful friend!" the prince whispered in his stallion's ear in the ancient language the horse understood. Ryen then reached back to retrieve the ornate cylinder carefully tied to his saddle.

By this time, the Royal Guard had formed a protective crescent around the prince, five rows deep. Fearlessly facing their squalidly clad foes with shields aglow from the light of the setting sun, every watchful eye of the Guard searched for even the slightest movement of threat. The well trained company was ever ready to spring to the defence of their beloved prince, and if necessary, to give their very lives in his defence.

Casually leaning back on a wooden structure that had quickly been assembled to resemble a throne of sorts, Awkmos acted neither surprised by the arrival of the prince, nor impressed by him and the well trained Hysperion. Internally, however, he cowered at the prince's unexpected display of confident authority and of this military discipline and precision.

## Tense Moments

With the cylinder firmly in hand, Ryen turned and for a moment paused, his eyes commanding the gaze of the dark ruler. Only Ryen noticed Awkmos briefly glance aside, avoiding the penetrating eyes of the prince. Only Ryen knew of the dark lord's unsettling discomfort with this piercing gaze and involuntary acknowledgement of the royal figure standing before him.

Slowly the prince advanced until he stood but a spear's length from the ruler of shadows. With a voice devoid of any fear, the prince announced firmly, "I bring a response from my father Rowen, most high king of this exalted realm!" The greeting was, once again, a thinly veiled reminder of his authority over the land upon which this wicked band had encamped. With eyes still fixed on Awkmos, Ryen unfastened the gold covered lid of the cylinder and reached in to retrieve the scroll it contained.

Consumed with impatience, Awkmos unexpectedly reached out for the beige coloured scroll, abruptly seizing it from Ryen's hand. With the speed of a storm cloud's flash, Cyrus drew his brilliant sword Flare. It shimmered in the evening light. With equal speed, the archers drew their bows as one man, with arrows set and ready to fly. Surprised by the quickness of this response, the dark enemies fumbled for a moment as they, in turn, drew their swords and readied arrows of their own. Unmoved by this sudden rousing and without even a glance back, the prince held up one hand of command, signalling to his men to secure their weapons. They obeyed the command instantly. The captain's sword went back into its scabbard and the archers' arrows back into their quivers. More reluctantly did the enemy do the same, wondering if perhaps they should strike. The evil lord slowly sat back wide-eyed, with scroll firmly in hand, realizing that his lamentable life had come within seconds of ending. He quickly wiped away a bead of sweat that rolled down the side of his already sweaty face.

## Chapter 18:

# The King's Reply

The heart of the dark lord raced as if in pursuit of his very last breath as he rushed to unroll the royal scroll. He abruptly brushed away the fly-infested remnants of his previous meal which still sat on the flat surface of a large stump set up as a makeshift table. Everything was sent crashing to the ground! Awkmos then laid the scroll down, stretching it out so he could read it with greater ease. In spite of the evil lord's failed attempt to capture the prince (for reasons which yet eluded him), King Rowen had still responded within three days, as demanded. "This fool of a king must have truly become misguided in allowing this message to be delivered by his very own son!" Awkmos secretly mused.

Holding up a smoking lamp to drive away the evening shadows from the scroll, Awkmos quickly mumbled to himself the words of the all important message as he hunched over the table. Slowly rising in jubilant realization, he broke out in a soft, yet disturbing laugh which grew increasingly louder, disturbing the evening stillness. Clenching the scroll between his black leather gloves, the sinister figure now stood tall. Raising it mockingly as if to make a royal announcement, he began for a second time to read the king's message, but loudly and more deliberately this time. Awkmos wanted everyone within the range of his fiendish voice to hear. The motley crowd pressed in, braving the protective crescent of the Guard, as they tried desperately to inch within hearing range. The Guard stirred, but held its ground. With characteristic, yet unmerited courtesy, the king's message was simple and brief.

*The King's Reply*

Rowen, High King of the Bright Realm
To Lord Awkmos,

Greetings! It remains my keenest desire and deepest hope that even the meekest and most needy of my royal realm would be spared any endangerment and not come to any harm by this threat of war that now overshadows my beloved land.

Therefore, in accordance with the ancient customs that forever bind regarding issues of war and peace, as High King of the Bright Realm, I offer you Astriel the Radiant, Guardian of the Realm and legendary sword of the kings of old.

Prove yourself a worthy and capable steward of this blade of legend, and the Bright Realm will be delivered over to you, for you to rule as you would so wish. Fail to rise to this worthiness, however, and the sword Astriel will return to its rightful king. Consequently, your dominion would henceforth be forfeited and forevermore end.

## Chapter 19:

# A Risky Surrender?

In a gesture of long-awaited victory, the dark ruler thrust the scroll high in triumph, parading it back and forth for every eye to see. A sudden wave of vicious jeers and scoffs raced through the dark encampment as news of Rowen's response spread like fire in dry brush. Laughing in disbelief almost, Awkmos sat back in wonder over what he had just read with his very own eyes. "This is indeed a welcomed turn of events, better than I could have ever planned!" he gloated ever so quietly to himself. Looking back defiantly at Prince Ryen, the dark one lied, "It was my conviction all along that your weakling of a father would not risk any harm to his precious little people if war were brought to his gate!" A second brutal wave of laughter and scoffing resounded throughout the evil encampment.

With narrowing eyes and serpent-like voice, Awkmos leaned forward in his chair towards Ryen until the scent of his sour breath reached the prince. Ryen resisted the urge to turn his head in search of fresher air, maintaining eye contact this deceiver. Irritated by the prince's undying confidence, the dark lord mocked with increasing boldness, "Now your highness! I suspect you must have with you an offering fitting this grand declaration. Perhaps a legendary token proving the sincerity of your father's wishes!?" Leaning away from Ryen, the ruler of shadows slumped defiantly back into his seat, arms crossed and head slightly to one side, his face displaying a sinister smirk and eyes defying the prince.

Stunned by the unexpected announcement, the Royal Guard looked on quizzically as their prince made his way back to his horse Braam. Unsure regarding the situation that was unfolding, the faithful stallion still stood at attention, ready to respond to any word of command from his master. Instead, the prince simply retrieved from concealment the longer object at the side of his saddle. Gracefully pulling it from its robes, the slender object glimmered, then shone brightly. The Hysperion had for so long revered the blade of legend, but had very rarely beheld it with their own eyes. Deep reverence and awe stirred among these men as they caught sight of Astriel the Radiant. A wave of fear quickly spread across the beach, however, among its enemies.

Rare had been the moments when any warrior beheld this champion of old, except during the raging battles of war. The very sight of Astriel inspired awe and confidence among those whose allegiance it held. Those whose allegiance the legendary blade did not hold, however, quaked with fear and quickly fell under its powerful stroke, defeated. Forged by the hands of the sages from an ancient steel, a metal so pure, it bore the appearance of glass but was light in weight and exceedingly strong. The double-handed grip of Astriel was made of skillfully carved ivory, laden with golden mesh and carefully fitted with a large, bright red gem on the end. The blade was etched with words from the ancient tongue of the sages, which not many could read or understand. The unsurpassed glory of Astriel was matched only by its legend. At this moment, it commanded the attention of every eye.

Ryen held the renowned blade sideways and slightly over his head for the Guard to behold. The prince could see wonder in the eyes of his brave men. He also perceived the disbelief of their minds and the despair of their hearts, for they perceived in a moment his intent. With a reassuring glance, he encouraged his men not to lose hope, but to trust.

Turning his attention back to the all-important matter at hand, Ryen slowly returned with the sword of the king now lying on outstretched hands before him to the impatient Awkmos, who had by this time risen to his feet. "Yesss! Yesss! Bring it to ME!" hissed the dark lord in disbelief. With wringing hands and bulging eyes fixed on the approaching blade, his evil heart drooled over this greatest of prizes.

Kneeling on one knee before Awkmos, the prince announced loudly and with obvious pride, "I present to you Astriel the Radiant, sword of Rowen, High King of the Bright Realm!" The gesture conveyed the surrender of a defeated king to his victor. With all his strength, the prince fought the urge to end this folly with one swift blow of the sword and deliver his beloved realm from the hand of this mocker. He chose instead to submit to the wisdom of his father, to believe the words of the sages, and to wait, instead, for a greater deliverance.

## Chapter 20:

# Know Your Enemy!

For years, King Rowen had carefully reflected upon the words of the sage concerning the darkness that would one day come to threaten the Bright Realm. Three days earlier, the weight of making the right choice concerning this threat lay squarely on his shoulders. And as broad as his shoulders were, this weight became almost unbearable. The king knew that the future of the Realm hung in the balance of his decision. Although it had been the most difficult decision he had ever had to make, Rowen was confident he had made the right one. He strongly suspected that the evil lord's lust for power and pursuit of glory and revenge would, without question, blind his already darkened judgment.

"In his greed, Awkmos will surely not pause long enough to consider the full meaning of the agreement placed before him," Rowen had confided to his son Ryen and to his faithful scribe and friend, Graphis. "His own great pride will befall him in the end! . . . I strongly suspect that, in the dark corners of his mind, Awkmos has already concluded that he IS Astriel's only true and worthy steward!" confidently concluded the king.

That, at least, is what the king had strongly hoped for. While still on one knee before the dark lord, it was also Ryen's hope. The defeat of the dark lord and the deliverance of the Bright Realm hinged entirely on what Awkmos would do next. For the briefest of moments, the prince wondered if perhaps his hope would prove to be but a misdirected dream long held by a long line of kings.

As it was the custom with kings and lords of that era long ago concerning the surrender of one ruler to another, Awkmos needed only to reach out and take for himself the offering placed before him, the sword of the king. The terms of the proposed agreement would henceforth become instantly and permanently binding to all those involved.

For a moment, still staring in unbelief, the dark lord's sinister eyes studied the majestic blade before him. Removing his black leather glove from his hand, he ran his long brutish fingers along the steel, as if to confirm by touch what his eyes beheld and mind struggled to believe.

With no further hesitation, however, Awkmos quickly gripped the sword by its ornate hilt, wrenching it from the hands of the waiting prince. With the terms of the agreement already well out of his mind, the evil lord raised the splendid sword to the sky with a loud and triumphal cry. "I am the NEW STEWARD of the sword!" he declared boastfully. "I am the NEW RULER of this land! . . . This kingdom is now MINE!" the dark lord shouted.

Instantly the evil army scattered across the beaches of the Ivory Shores resounding with deafening cries of triumph and malice. Remaining calm, the Hysperion held their defensive formation around the prince, every eye scanning intently for a treacherous move.

When the waves of snarls, barks and jeers had settled, the dark lord slowly turned his gaze toward the prince. Ryen, who had risen to his feet and, out of caution, had taken a step back, stood calmly before Awkmos, unsure of his intent. It was quickly revealed, however. Pointing his newly acquired symbol of authority at the prince, the evil ruler snarled, "As the NEW ruler of this pitiful land, hear, now, my first command to YOU!" He made no attempt to conceal his obvious pleasure over this sudden gain of authority. "Leave me now, Insolence!" he proudly ordered. Yellow phlegm spewed out of his foul mouth, dropping on his bearded chin. "Go and make ready MY throne! After MY earliest convenience, I will come to claim MY kingdom!"

## Chapter 21:

# Doubts and Fear

In spite of the defeat of the people of Mangled Mountain, Prince Ryen did not want to, again, risk taking the treacherous mountain path for their journey back. In spite of the urgency he felt to return promptly to his father's side with his report of Awkmos' response, he also valued the life of every man under his command.

"Such a risk is not necessary," confided the prince to Captain Cyrus, who rode once again at his side. The two men had exchanged very few words with each other since having left the Ivory Shores . . . and the sword of the king behind. Few words were necessary. The surrender of the legendary blade to Awkmos had taken the entire Hysperion, including Cyrus, unawares. While trapped at the top of Mangled Mountain, however, the brave captain had learned not to despair, but to trust his master's wisdom and will. Questions concerning Astriel the Radiant threatened to wrap themselves around his mind and heart, like the constricting coils of a large serpent. He chose, however, to slay that serpent and release himself of its deadly coils by once again trusting the prince.

"We will take the route south of Mangled Mountain, pass the northern base of the High Peaks of Nesheer, until we reach the Swift River! We will then follow the river home to Tyra-Migdal," the prince finally clarified to the captain. The way past the High Peaks and along the river would still add days to the company's return trek, and time for each man to think, to ponder. Because it also passed through the domain of the Kanaff, the white giants of the sky, ever watchful guardians of the southern regions of the Realm, their trek home would not of necessity be free of peril.

The trek south continued long and silent, one day on into the next. Each member of the Guard became lost in his own thoughts. The Kanaff, however, granted unhindered passage to the

*Doubts and Fear*

weary travellers, recognizing from afar the company as people of the Realm. So the party travelled on.

The campfires flickered brightly along the bank of the Swift River as the exhausted company, wrapped in their saddle blankets, gathered around the flames to stay warm. It was the Guard's last encampment before they arrived at Tyra-Migdal the next day. However, the men were still deeply troubled over what they had witnessed on the Ivory Shores.

Prince Ryen knew his men as a caring shepherd would know his sheep. The trouble that was making their hearts heavy did not escape him. Like brothers were these men to the prince. When they finally approached him long after the sun had set, he openly welcomed them to his campfire. "My lord!" they eagerly implored. "We would desire to understand the events on the beach, for our hearts have not rested since having left that evil nest of vipers days ago!"

Each weary and yearning heart leaned in with anticipation, waiting for their good master's reply. "Brothers!" the prince started slowly. "Surely do I understand what troubles your hearts.

If it had not been for the promise of a greater deliverance, I would have at that very moment lopped the head off the shoulders of that fiendish mocker. For such was the fire that threatened to consume my breast!" Ryen looked intently into the eyes of each man surrounding his campfire. They saw blazing in his eyes an even greater fire! "But do not let this brief trouble snuff out the embers of hope that still remain in your hearts, my brothers!" he added reassuringly. "Soon the entire Realm will understand, your trouble will turn to joy, and your hope shall be rewarded."

Though their understanding of the events on the beach was not any greater, the words of their master of a soon-coming joy filled the Guard with comfort and peace. The weary men rested peacefully that night, no longer heavy of heart and with renewed hope in the promise of a greater deliverance.

## Chapter 22:

# Well Done!

"Everything came about as you had suspected!" the prince reported with enthusiasm to his weary father. "Awkmos took for himself the sword Astriel, and in doing so, blindly accepted the terms of the agreement set before him!"

The heavy heart of the king was suddenly relieved by his son's glad tidings! Though Rowen had been confident in his suspicions concerning the dark lord and the proposed agreement, his heart still battled the heavy blood surging through his veins as the king eagerly waited for Ryen's return. The wait seemed to have added years of age to the king's features.

"Well done!" the king proudly exclaimed. "Well done indeed!" he added, finally satisfied.

*Tales of the Bright Realm*

"Most glad are these tidings that confirm what my heart already knew!" continued Rowen relieved. With hands folded at his back, the king paced dreamlike back and forth along the lengths of bear hides lying before his throne. To some distant realm of long ago he appeared to have been carried off in his thoughts.

Stopping finally before the prince, Rowen spoke confidently, "My son, long have we awaited the Great Day of Deliverance, when the Bright Realm would be forevermore freed from the threat of all evil!" The king's words resonated with the heart of the the prince, like the quiet waves of a healing sea splashing gently onto troubled shores. Rowen continued, "Long have we awaited the fulfilment of the ancient promise!" His voice had filled with hope and anticipation. Softly, the king led into the words of an ancient, sacred song, singing in the tongue of the kings of old:

> Darkness descended, white shores, mountains and plains
> Dark shadows increased, realm of light they would reign
> Words of the sages, a final battle unleashed

> A victor as promised, from scabbard unsheathed
> By might and by power blade of light shall deliver
> From all darkness at last, defeated forever

Ryen understood this ancient tongue, for he had learned it as boy in his father's presence. Though the prince had never before heard the song, his heart had grasped its meaning, even when hidden in such mystery. And his heart rejoiced in the hearing of it! However, an urgent matter concerning the people of the Realm at this time needed swift attention.

"Father!" The single word interrupted the tranquillity of this reverent moment. "Our people have been giving ear to dark tidings concerning the evil lord Awkmos on our shores, and of the reported peril of Astriel." Ryen paused a moment to allow his father time to take in the meaning of these less than joyful tidings. After a moment, the prince continued, "Their hearts are sorely troubled by these fearful tidings and in need of much quieting." Ryen paused again with his gaze on his father. "Father," he continued with urgency, "let us bring to them the good tidings we have at this moment shared together. Our people have a need of hearing the ancient words of the sage! Let us now care for them in their trouble!"

In need of no urging, the king nodded in full agreement, sharing his son's concerns for the distressed people of the Realm. His heart was grieved, however, at hearing about this trouble. "My son!" the king finally spoke with renewed determination and singleness of mind. "Send word to every corner of our great realm. Seven days hence we shall gather in the Great Court of Assembly! . . . The time has indeed come for the people of the Bright Realm to, once again, hear the ancient words of the sage!"

## Chapter 23:

# The Great Assembly

The Great Court of Assembly was a very large grassy area inside the castle walls, in the main court area. Leading up to the meeting place was a wide stone walkway lined on both sides by the white figures of ancient kings. Each kingly shape was adorned in armour, standing proudly, sword in hand and raised in battle or in triumph! Among the kings stood the figures of Victor the Valiant, Thoren the Truthful, and Fabian the Faithful. The people marvelled greatly at the sight of these great guardians of the Realm as the crowd made its way towards the court. They marvelled even more at the glorious accounts of yesteryear each figure recounted.

Banners displaying the royal colours and symbols surrounded the meeting place, fluttering peacefully in the gentle breeze. All were present who could come in response to the request of their king. The Kanaff, the kingdom's feathered servants, had quickly delivered his urgent message to every corner of the Bright Realm. Those living afar who dared took flight on the backs or in the talons of the giant white birds, racing through clouds and over mountain passages and peaks. Their courage was rewarded by this rarest of glimpses of the glorious Realm to which they belonged.

All stood in awe and wonder at the sight of their arrival, as traveller after traveller, at times alone, at times in small groups, was deposited in the middle of the court by these majestic birds. Their piercing shrieks would for a moment render useless the ears of anyone too near as each giant bird flew off to gather more travellers. The wind from their great wings would send sprawling anything not secured to the ground and anyone unsuspecting, to the amusement of the growing crowd! This amazing spectacle went on from early morning and into the greater part of the day. None tired of the sight of it!

*The Great Assembly*

Throughout the day, distant neighbours would exchange lingering questions and concerns about what they had seen and heard. "Why this urgent assembly?" some wondered. "The dark lord must be moving upon us!" others pondered. Still others told of strange beings crossing their lands, as friends, neighbours and countrymen came together in the Great Court of Assembly.

Finally, as the afternoon grew long, the time came for the king and his son to ascend the wooden structure built especially for this gathering. The eager crowd erupted instantly with joyful applause and cheers. "King Rowen forever! Prince Ryen forevermore!" echoed off the walls and throughout the inner courts of the castle. This exaltation would have kept on for much longer had Ryen not beckoned the crowd for silence as he spoke first, acknowledging the people's fears and concerns. "Beloved subjects of the Realm," he concluded, "harken, now, to the words of my father and your king, Rowen, High King of the Bright Realm!"

The king waited in gratitude for the jubilation to quiet before finally beginning. "Long ago, late one stormy night, when I had just come into my reign as king over the Realm," Rowen started, "an unexpected visitor came knocking at the great gates of Tyra-Migdal. The visitor was requesting a meeting with the king, stating it was a matter of extreme importance!" The king's voice rang out clearly, commanding the ear of his audience. A deafening silence had come over the crowd as they listened to this tale of intrigue from the past. "This visitor from long ago," continued Rowen, voice echoing off the court walls, "was none other than the great Sophim, wise sage of old!" The assembled stirred with awe at the mention of this legendary figure and needed settling before their king could continue.

"Sophim spoke of a reign of peace and prosperity that would one day come to the Realm," Rowen reminded his people. "He also warned of a great peril, a darkness that would one day arise to threaten the very existence of the Bright Realm." An uneasy agitation rippled through the crowd at these foreboding words. The king continued, however. "That fateful night long ago, the sage bestowed upon me a timely and most precious gift—a sword which I had for unending years longed to behold, but had been lost in the

Battle of Appolumi—Astriel the Radiant!" Upon hearing of the blade of legend, the agitation of the crowd gave way to a deep sense of wonder.

The king quickly brought his listeners back to order and to the purpose of his tale, pausing to call to attention each listener. "That night, before leaving," continued Rowen, "the sage counselled earnestly, 'This blade shall guard the realm of a worthy steward only! Value your people above all else, and your kingdom the blade shall deliver and establish forever!' "

## Chapter 24:

# Be Still!

Like a child caught up in a story of peril and intrigue, the assembled listened with keen interest and attention to King Rowen as his tale led up to the arrival of the dark lord, the evil messenger, the ultimatum, and the threat of war and invasion. The crowd gasped with one breath when hearing about the surrender of Astriel, for all hope of deliverance had appeared to have been lost in the surrendering of the blade of legend. Dismay immediately began to rise within the listeners at their cries of despair and woe, like a flock of sheep abandoned to the terrors of the night.

As king, Rowen did not need to explain his decision to the people of the Realm. However, neither did he desire for his people to remain any longer in the shadows concerning the coming of Awkmos, for he loved them as his own children. The king had anticipated this frightful response, for he knew his people well. They would not easily understand, but would they trust him?

Like the sound of distant thunder heralding the coming of heavy rain, the king's voice suddenly resounded, "My beloved!" Patiently Rowen waited for the agitation to lessen. Once again the king's appeal went out, this time with the calming reassurance of a father to his frightened child, "My beloved!" One by one, the agitated responded to this loving appeal. The gaze of young and old was once again fixed on their king. Everyone had again become still and was waiting! Their beloved ruler stood before them, arms opened as in a father's welcoming embrace. His eyes, filled with loving concern, with tenderness and kindness, were upon them. No other words were uttered by the ruler. No other words were needed.

*Be Still!*

Like the buzz of angry bees, a growing commotion began to stir. No sooner had the assembled begun to wonder about this untimely intrusion than the back of the crowd started to part as the noise of hushes and whisperings started to build. Like a ship parting a heavy night mist, a tall gray figure with an even taller walking staff slowly moved through the crowd toward the wooden structure. The people closed in behind, in the wake of the passing figure, wondering at this strange intruder. Their wonder would have been even greater had they known about the long slender object concealed under the intruder's gray woollen cloak.

## CHAPTER 25:

# A Tale of Deliverance

The palace guard reacted instinctively to the sudden threat of this unknown intruder. In well trained discipline, with shields raised and spears lowered, the men quickly moved in, between the king and this somber figure. With eyes raised toward Prince Ryen, who had been standing at the king's side all the while, the principal guard waited for a command of action. However, no such command was given! Instead, the countenance of the prince grew warm, as he recognized an old friend.

"Forgive me, my lords, for the manner of my intrusion!" The strange figure finally spoke. His voice was as the roar of a rushing waterfall, loud for all to hear. Yet, it was as graceful as the sound of the summer wind rustling gently through the trees, full of quietness and mystery. At once, an unusual calm came over the assembled, as if all were swept away on a cloud of serenity and tranquillity.

"Welcome, my beloved friend!" joyfully spoke the king as he, too, recognized the familiar figure. As this *friend* of the king's pushed back the hood covering his eyes, the anxious crowd was finally able to see who was this one, now a beloved friend of the king. "Please, come! Join us at our side, my dearest Sophim!" The crowd gasped in wonder as the sage started up the stairs of the structure to join the king and prince.

Arriving at the king's side, the ancient one announced slyly, "Great and glad tidings do I bring concerning the Bright Realm, your majesties! If I may?" Gesturing toward his assembled people, the king gave his friend the sage permission to address the crowd.

The royal banners surrounding the Great Court of Assembly danced softly in the warm evening breeze. Bouncing off the faces of the assembled was the glittering light of the many torches Prince Ryen had ordered lit for this all important gathering. The sun had already set on the Bright Realm.

The sage started earnestly into the telling of his dangerous journey up Mangled Mountain, his battle with the people of the mountain, and the saving of the trapped Hysperion. Prince Ryen was pleased with this recounting. The need for haste had left no time for the telling of the arrival of Sophim on the mountain.

In captivated amazement, the people listened to the telling of these recent events as Sophim continued, "Lord Awkmos considered himself, indeed, to be the worthy steward of the blade of legend. But at the end of this uncertain era, his true unworthiness has been assuredly revealed!" The people stood silently, riveted to this tale of wonders.

Finally, in his retelling, the sage arrived at the most important part of the tale—the deliverance of Astriel. He confirmed that the dark ruler's own pride and desire for power had led to his defeat and ultimate desolation. "By accepting the sword of the king," he added, voice echoing throughout the court, "the dark lord not only sealed his own fate, but the fate of all evil." Sophim paused, allowing time for these last words to enter the minds of his listeners, then continued. "For other evils desired the sword Astriel for themselves, to be the uncontested steward of the blade and ruler over all domains!" The assembly was held tightly in the grasp of every word. "Alas, the dark army of Awkmos turned on their master, however. And while they warred against each other, the shadowy creatures of every field, forest, hill, and mountain moved upon Awkmos and his evil hordes. The blade of legend drew them until every evil of every kind had gathered on the white shores of the Realm!" Pausing again, Sophim waited.

Young and old stood as if icebound, captivated by the telling of this amazing tale of deliverance. "The evil battle raged on among these fiendish foes!" resumed the sage with increased fervour. "Finally, thinking to wield it against his enemy and secure his victory, the dark lord raised the majestic blade to the sky!"

Like a lion eyeing its prey, Sophim peered intently into events which no other eye could see. Looking! Waiting! Then finally, "Lo, the blade of legend would not be wielded by an unworthy

## A Tale of Deliverance

steward! As the dark one held the sword high, the ancient light of Astriel the Radiant began to be revealed! Dimly at first! Then in ever increasing radiance! Its wonder commanded every evil eye present to behold its light! When the brightness of the blade had reached its fullness, . . ." pausing, with his gaze intently on this epic battle as it unfolded before him, the sage declared with thundering emphasis, "the full glory of Astriel shone forth! . . . In one final and fatal moment, all evil came to its ruin, . . . instantly consumed where they stood by the pure light of the great Deliverer!" Pausing again, the expression of the sage lightened, as the historic scene faded from his view. "Thus has the sword of legend forever defeated all evil!" Sophim added as he brought the retelling of the tale of wonders to its victorious end.

Standing silently for a moment, and filled with an unspeakable joy, Sophim slowly turned his gaze again toward the people now overcome with wonder and amazement. "I found the blade of legend standing alone, in peace and in victory in the white sand of the shores of the Realm, . . . from whence I retrieved it!"

"From whence I retrieved it!" All wondered at the meaning of these last, trailing words of the sage. But before anyone could wonder for much longer, the ancient servant of the Realm declared earnestly, "For unending ages has my heart yearned for this day, to declare with full assurance to the people throughout the Bright Realm, and to its king and prince, the glorious proclamation long awaited by generations of kings, of men, and of all other creatures from ages past. What was designed in the Ancient Age, on this day of days has assuredly come to pass!" the sage finally declared. Sophim glanced at his dear friends, the king and prince, and then back to the awaiting crowd. "Evil," he thundered, "has now . . . and forevermore . . . been vanquished! . . . All who belong to this great and glorious realm may henceforth and forevermore freely go forth and revel in the joy of the new age of the Great Day of Perfect Rest!" The crowd erupted with cries of joy and praise for the Great Design of the Ancient Age.

## Chapter 26:

# Jubilation

Up to this moment, Sophim had kept hidden the long and slender object concealed at his side. Beckoning the crowd to come to order and turning back to the king, the aged one declared with obvious enthusiasm, "I believe I have in my possession, oh king, an heirloom of great value belonging to you and your house!" With no further delays, throwing back his heavy cloak and pulling out the object from concealment, Sophim fell to one knee before the king and held it up with both hands for the ruler to behold. "A king cannot reign without his sword!" he expressed softly to his friend as he looked up at Rowen. Across his outstretched hands rested Astriel the Radiant, Deliverer of the Bright Realm.

*Tales of the Bright Realm*

Amazed, but not in unbelief, Rowen carefully received his sword from the hands of the sage, while the prince looked on, heart full of joy! Turning to his people with Astriel resting in his outstretched hands, with thanksgiving the king lifted his gaze to the sky. Looking back to the great sword, eyes beholding the gleaming blade as if for the first time, the king's countenance suddenly became flooded with glorious light. At that moment, he witnessed in the blade, as if having suddenly travelled back through the ages himself, the glory of the Bright Realm. The vision was from as far back as could be beheld, to the very foundation of the Realm, to the first king and the Ancient Age. The tales of the Realm unfolded before his very eyes, from that beginning, up to this day of days and far into the future, where the eye could no longer behold, but where the heart knew of yet even greater glory. For a lasting moment, the dark night sky was alight with the brightness of the glory of the blade. Night became like full day. The king basked in the radiance of Astriel, while the entire assembly witnessed its brightness.

## Jubilation

Just as suddenly as it had been revealed, the glory that shone forth returned to the blade of wonders. Beholding with amazement the last flickers of glory, King Rowen helped his beloved friend back to his feet. Then, raising the majestic Astriel in triumph towards the heavens, the king's voice rang out, "Behold, Astriel the Radiant, great Deliverer, Guardian and Sustainer of the Bright Realm!"

Standing in stupefied awe and fear of the glory they had just witnessed, now at the sight of the amazing blade of legend, the entire assembly instantly resounded with shouts and cheers of jubilation which filled the Great Court of Assembly and the night sky. So great was their jubilation on that day of days that the sound rushed over the court walls like a mighty wave, down the mountain on every side, flooding the narrow streets of the villages below. By the power of Astriel, the jubilant sound rushed on in every direction into the fields, woodlands and deep forested regions of the land. For a moment, every beast and living creature in its wake stood still, listening in awed silence to this unfathomable sound of celebration coming to them on the winds from the city. And they understood the meaning of it.

Suddenly caught up in this great wave of jubilation, the creatures themselves began to dance and sing, while others jumped and pranced. Still others flapped and flew, every creature entering into this joyful celebration in its own way.

As the great festive wave from Tyra-Migdal receded, in return it carried in its wake the jubilant reply of the creatures of the Realm, flowing back through the deep forested regions, through the woodlands and fields and into the narrow village streets, up the mountain sides and back over the court walls. The entire assembly for a moment stood still, listening to this jubilant sound coming to them on the winds from every corner of the Realm. And they understood the meaning of it.

Astriel the Radiant had returned to Tyra-Migdal and to its rightful steward. The Bright Realm would henceforth and forevermore be a land of perfect rest. Its people would be free! Free to live with no fear of darkness. Free to travel to and explore other realms with no concerns of the shadows or evil. Free to declare their deepest

*Jubilation*

and undying devotion to their king and prince, to whom they would forever remain loyal and true. Free to forever live as intended since the Ancient Age as people of this glorious Realm, to wherever their desires would lead them and whatever adventure their hearts would aspire.

All through the night and into the early morning, wave upon wave of jubilation flowed out from the castle city. Wave upon jubilant wave receded back from the Realm, in endless rounds of exaltation. Since the foundation of the Bright Realm, every king and prince of ages past, every subject and creature of old deeply longed for the coming of the Day of Perfect Rest. That day had finally arrived! Never before had anyone beheld such jubilation! Never before had there been such a cause for celebration!

## Chapter 27:

# The Decree

As the waters of any great wave eventually settle and once again become calm, so did the jubilation of that day. To insure that the people of his kingdom would never forget this day of days, King Rowen decreed an entire month of festivities throughout every province and township of the Bright Realm. He also decreed that every subject of the realm was to take part in this grand celebration, to which they did and gladly!

All were to tend only to daily tasks of necessity (or whenever possible, to tend to no task at all) for the entire month of celebrations. Not only did the king provide for every festivity need. He also cared for any losses his loyal subjects might have suffered in their month-long participation.

*Tales of the Bright Realm*

Once a year from that day forward, a month of festivities was held, beginning on the very day of the defeat of evil. King Rowen called the occasion the Celebration of Deliverance. Even the creatures of land, forest and sky celebrated together, in harmony and peace, each kind in its own way. To make this possible, through the power of Astriel, the king suspended the natural instincts of each creature for the duration of the festivities. Throughout the Realm, this unnatural reprieve became a wonder every subject desired to behold. Together, men and women young and old soon entered into the celebration with the creatures of the Realm, for King Rowen had further decreed that every inhabitant of the Bright Realm should learn the ancient tongue of the kings. Their jubilation turned to fellowship as the kingdom folks celebrated with the creatures of the Realm. The fellowship that had once been lost in ages past had now been restored. This became an even greater wonder to behold. Year after year afterwards, the Bright Realm in its entirety participated in the Celebration of Deliverance together.

After this first month of festivities had come to an end, the people who had assembled in the castle courts to celebrate returned with great joy to their towns and villages. They again took up their daily tasks with delight, grateful for being subjects of this great realm and its perfect rest.

Epilogue:
# The Glory of the Realm

King Rowen's kingdom continued to prosper under his rule, with the wise counsel of his dearest friends Graphis the scribe and Sophim the sage. Graphis gladly welcomed the appointment of Sophim as main adviser to the king. Prince Ryen became co-ruler alongside his father. Together, their rule of the Bright Realm led to even greater prosperity and peace. Cyrus was promoted from Captain of the Guard to General of the entire Royal Army, a position of service he humbly, but most gratefully accepted.

As the kingdom prospered, the king revised his decree for the yearly celebrations to be extended. At first, one month of celebrations became two. Then, two months became four, after which four became six. In time, the festivities became a year-long celebration of the Day of Deliverance. One celebration would lead right into the next, until time became unimportant. Daily tasks became part of the celebrations, no longer viewed as tasks, but as acts of gratitude to their king. The natural instincts of the creatures of the realm were permanently suspended so that they lived with each other in constant peace and harmony, their very nature changed so that every creature was now sustained by the nourishment from the fertile ground of the Realm.

Soon, the people of Mangled Mountain joined the celebrations out of gratitude for the gracious invitation of the king. They too gladly became subjects of the Bright Realm and all marvelled at such grace. That entire chain of mountains was renamed Hills of Wonder, for their treacherous peaks had returned to the ground from whence they came, allowing for safe travel that way of the kingdom folks. The *throwing trees* of the former mountain were given a new name and a new purpose. The Trees became known as the Trees of Lore, for they provided the refreshment of shade while they recounted the long and glorious history of the Realm to travellers passing

*The Glory of the Realm*

through those parts. The travellers were able to understand the language of the Trees, having learned the ancient tongue of the kings.

Many travelled to the area they once knew as the Windy Plains far to the north to behold the rebirth of the Arid Lands, which had been renamed New Flora. The sages had long ago foretold that this land would one day flourish with plants and vegetation of a beauty that the people had never before beheld. This region now stood proudly above all others, its luscious appearance beyond compare and even imagination.

Along with this prosperity, the Bright Realm increased in glory from year to year, from glory to glory every year. Tyra-Migdal, the castle city, also grew in splendour. Its white stone became the brightest of marble, trimmed with every kind of precious stone. From every corner of the Bright Realm, the people of the land beheld the glory of Tyra-Migdal.

After a great many more years, time itself was forgotten. Astriel the Radiant, blade of legend, was placed in a glass-like encasement in the Great Chamber of Light, a chamber built of the same clear steel that Astriel was made of, and sat at the very top of the High Tower of the Kings. The light of Astriel shone brightly throughout the entire realm so that there was no longer any night. Thus was fulfilled the final ancient words concerning the Bright Realm.

---

King Rowen's stewardship of the sword did prove to be worthy, true and pure in heart. The glory of the Bright Realm surpassed any other realm that had ever been known. Never had any realm been so glorious or known such prosperity and peace as that of King Rowen's and Prince Ryen's. Never had any sword been so mighty in life and in legend as Astriel the Radiant, Guardian and Deliverer of the Bright Realm. And to think, it all started with an unexpected visit (but not unplanned) by a wise and humble servant of a young king and a tale of a mysterious sword on that fateful night long, long ago. Who knew ever could there have been or ever could there be such a glorious realm?

# *The Glory of the Realm*

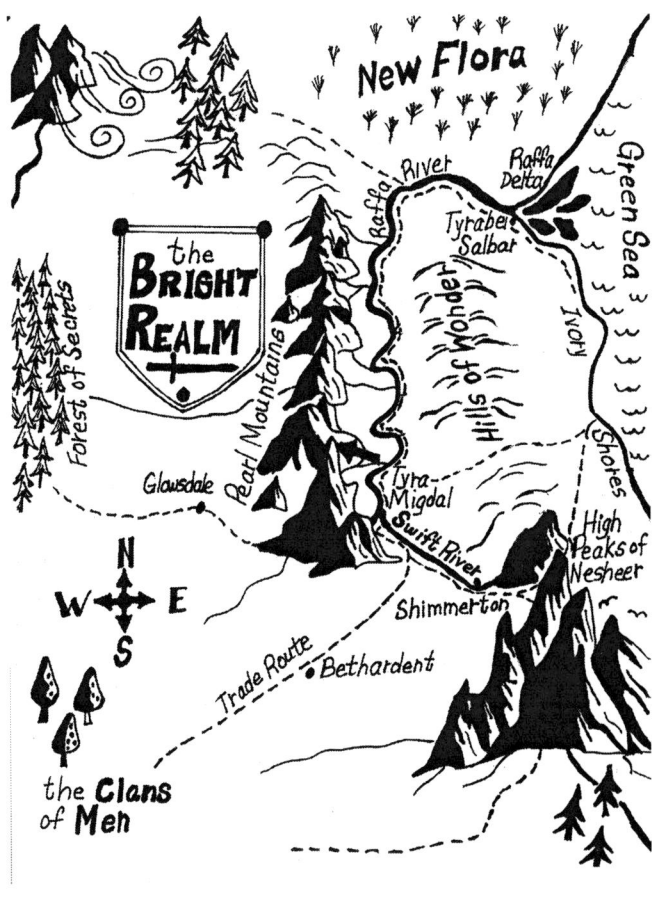

BE LOOKING FOR
## BOOK 2
in the series
TALES OF THE BRIGHT REALM
# "THE STONES OF PROMISE"

---

Prince Ryen was trapped! Unable to move forward! Unable to retreat! Whoever had launched such a large spear had chosen the perfect place for his ambush! He must have known this terrain very well!

Exhausted! Hungry! And for the first time in his life really, fearful! He wondered if it had been a mistake for him and Cyrus to set off on such a perilous mission! He had been confident of their success, for Sophim was to accompany them. "Surely we have nothing to fear!" he remembered half jesting with Cyrus over the General's objections to the Counsel's choice of only the three of them for such an important assignment:

the retrieval of the Stones of Promise. But where was Sophim now? And Cyrus? He had been separated from the Sage and the General three days earlier, as they travelled along the Valley of Mists. The mysterious mist that had suddenly enveloped them was so thick, he had gotten turned around and confused. A mistake an inexperienced warrior may have easily committed. But not the Prince! And surely not on this mission!

His heart ached desperately for the familiar, for his home at the highest peak of the Pearl Mountains, at the center of the glorious Bright Realm. . . . "The glory of the Realm," he pondered within himself. The prince wondered if there would be any glory left in the Realm, in Astriel, by the time he returns, if he returns at all.

Somewhere in the Forest of Secrets, the Stones of Promise had seen sent away long ago by the Counsel of Sages to be hidden, safe from the threat of evil. Now they were needed! Desperately! Somehow the Prince had to find the Stones and return them to the Realm before it was loo late. The future and perhaps the very existence of the Bright Realm depended on his success!

CPSIA information can be obtained at www.ICGtesting.com
Printed in the USA
LVOW10s1053101214

418035LV00010B/95/P